The World's Continents

EUROPE

Polly Goodman

HODDER
Wayland

an imprint of Hodder Children's Books

The World's Continents series includes:

Cover and title page images: Satellite photographs of Europe taken from space, which have been specially coloured on a computer.

Contents page: A satellite photograph of Europe, taken from a different position in space.

Europe is a simplified and updated version of the title *Europe* in Wayland's *Continents* series.

Text copyright © 2000 Hodder Wayland
Volume copyright © 2000 Hodder Wayland

First published in Great Britain in 1996 by Wayland Publishers Ltd. This simplified and updated edition published in 2000 by Hodder Wayland, an imprint of Hodder Children's Books.

A Catalogue record for this book is available from the British Library.

ISBN 0 7502 2867 9

Printed and bound in Italy by G. Canale & C. S.p.A.

Hodder Children's Books
A division of Hodder Headline plc
338 Euston Road, London NW1 3BH

Statistics
Population figures in this book are for 1998.

Sources
Eurostat, 1995
United Nations Development Programme
Unicef: *The State of the World's Children, 2000*

Picture Credits
All Sports 26; Britstock-IFA 14, 37; Camera Press 16, 35; Format 22; Gamma 21, 34; Hulton Deutsch 18, 19; Hutchinson 20, 42; Impact 40; Image Bank 23, 27; Military Picture Library 43; Panos 40; Dr. J. Rowe 41; Science Photo Library 1, 3, 9, 12, 39; Trip 8, 10, 11, 13, 25, 29, 30, 31, 32, 33, 35, 36, 38; Zefa 26.

Map artwork by Peter Bull. Graph artwork by Mark Whitchurch. Globe artwork by Tim Mayer.

CONTENTS

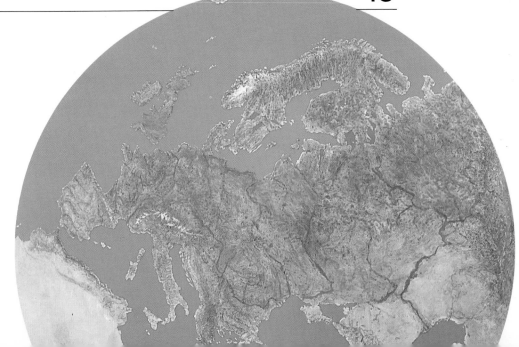

COUNTRIES OF EUROPE

NORTH-WEST EUROPE

FINLAND
Area: 338,145 km²
Population: 5,154,000
Main languages: Finnish, Swedish

NORWAY
Area: 323,378 km²
Population: 4,419,000
Language: Norwegian

SWEDEN
Area: 444,964 km²
Population: 8,875,000
Main language: Swedish

ICELAND
Area: 103,000 km²
Population 276,000
Main language: Icelandic

DENMARK
Area: 43,092 km²
Population: 5,270,000
Languages: Danish, Faerose

UNITED KINGDOM
Area: 244,100 km²
Population: 58,649,000
Main languages: English, Welsh, Gaelic

BELGIUM
Area: 30,519 km²
Population: 10,141,000
Main language: Flemish

EIRE
Area: 70,283 km²
Population: 3,681,000
Main languages: Irish, English

LUXEMBOURG
Area: 2,586 km²
Population: 422,000
Main languages: Letzeburgish, French

FRANCE
Area: 543,965 km²
Population: 58,683,000
Main languages: French (Breton and Basque minorities)

GERMANY
Area: 356,945km²
Population: 82,133,000
Main language: German

AUSTRIA
Area: 83,853 km²
Population: 8,140,000
Main language: German

NETHERLANDS
Area: 41,863 km²
Population: 15,678,000
Main language: Dutch

MONACO
Area: 1.8 km²
Population: 33,000
Main languages: French, Monagasque

SWITZERLAND
Area: 41,288 km²
Population: 7,299,000
Main languages: German, French, Italian, Romansch

LIECHTENSTEIN
Area: 160 km²
Population: 32,000
Main language: German

Map labels:
Reykjavik
ICELAND
0 200 400 600 800 km
0 100 200 300 400 500 miles
SWEDEN   FINLAND
Helsinki
NORWAY
Oslo   Stockholm
NORTHERN
IRELAND
Dublin   UNITED
EIRE   KINGDOM
DENMARK
Copenhagen
London
NETHERLANDS
Berlin
Amsterdam
Brussels   GERMANY
BELGIUM
Paris
LUXEMBOURG
FRANCE   Vienna
SWITZERLAND   AUSTRIA
Bern
LIECHTENSTEIN
MONACO

CENTRAL AND EASTERN EUROPE

The countries of central and eastern Europe were under communist control until 1989–90.

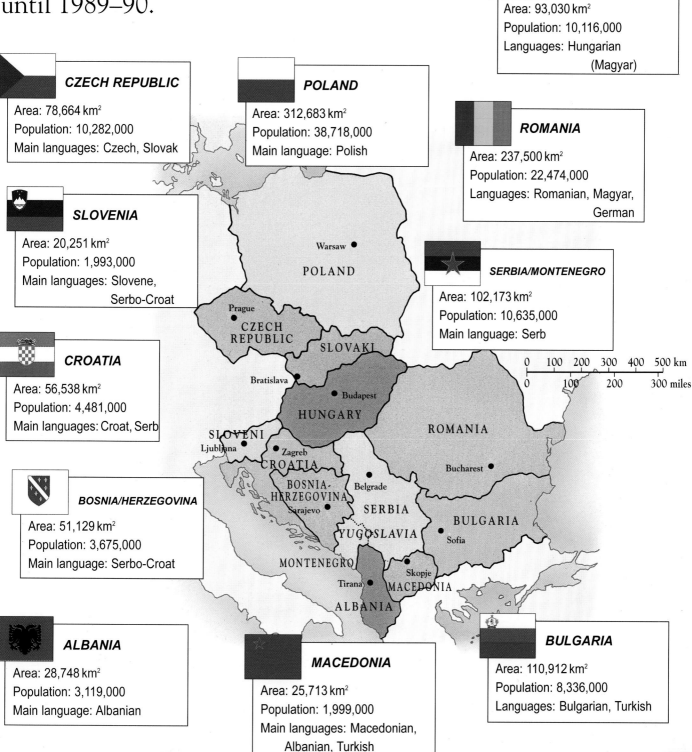

SLOVAKIA
Area: 49,035 km²
Population: 5,377,000
Languages: Slovak, Magyar

HUNGARY
Area: 93,030 km²
Population: 10,116,000
Languages: Hungarian
(Magyar)

CZECH REPUBLIC
Area: 78,664 km²
Population: 10,282,000
Main languages: Czech, Slovak

POLAND
Area: 312,683 km²
Population: 38,718,000
Main language: Polish

ROMANIA
Area: 237,500 km²
Population: 22,474,000
Languages: Romanian, Magyar,
German

SLOVENIA
Area: 20,251 km²
Population: 1,993,000
Main languages: Slovene,
Serbo-Croat

SERBIA/MONTENEGRO
Area: 102,173 km²
Population: 10,635,000
Main language: Serb

CROATIA
Area: 56,538 km²
Population: 4,481,000
Main languages: Croat, Serb

BOSNIA/HERZEGOVINA
Area: 51,129 km²
Population: 3,675,000
Main language: Serbo-Croat

ALBANIA
Area: 28,748 km²
Population: 3,119,000
Main language: Albanian

MACEDONIA
Area: 25,713 km²
Population: 1,999,000
Main languages: Macedonian,
Albanian, Turkish

BULGARIA
Area: 110,912 km²
Population: 8,336,000
Languages: Bulgarian, Turkish

0 100 200 300 400 500 km
0   100   200   300 miles

SOUTHERN EUROPE

Southern Europe's climate is influenced by the Mediterranean Sea, which helps support a major tourist industry.

PORTUGAL

Area: 92,389 km²
Population: 9,869,000
Languages: Portuguese

SPAIN

Area: 504,782 km²
Population: 39,628,000
Languages: Spanish, Castilian, Catalan, Basque, Galician

ITALY

Area: 301,287 km²
Population: 57,369,000
Languages: Italian (German, French, Albanian minorities)

GREECE

Area: 131,944 km²
Population:10,600,000
Languages: Greek

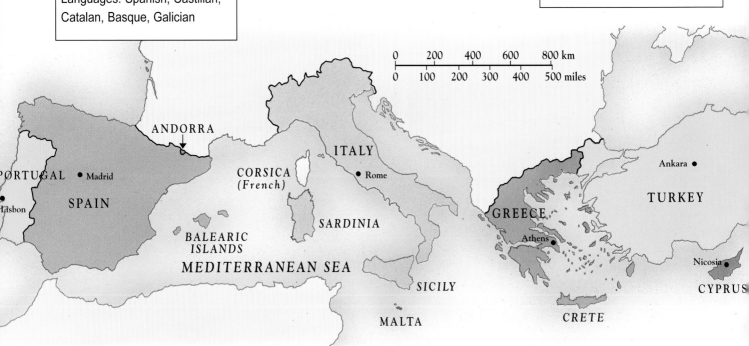

MALTA

Area: 316 km²
Population: 384,000
Languages: Maltese, English

TURKEY

Area: 779,452 km²
Population: 64,479,000
Languages: Turkish, Kurdish

CYPRUS

Area: 9,251 km²
Population: 771,000
Languages: Greek, Turkish

RUSSIAN FEDERATION AND THE CIS

In 1991, the Soviet Union split up into independent countries, some of which formed the Commonwealth of Independent States (CIS), and the Russian Federation.

EUROPEAN RUSSIA

Area: 17,675,400 km²
Population: 147,434,000
Languages: Russian, Tatar, Ukrainian, Chuvash, Bashkan, Belarussian, Chechen

ESTONIA

Area: 45,100 km²
Population:1,429,000
Languages: Estonian, Russian

LATVIA

Area: 64,589 km²
Population: 2,242,000
Languages: Lettish, Russian
Belarussian

LITHUANIA

Area: 65,200 km²
Population: 3,694,000
Languages: Lithuanian, Russian
Polish

BELARUS

Area: 207,600 km²
Population: 10,315,000
Languages: Belarussian,
Russian, Polish

UKRAINE

Area: 603,700 km²
Population: 50,861,000
Languages: Ukrainian, Russian
Belarussian

GEORGIA

Area: 69,700 km²
Population: 5,059,000
Languages: Georgian, Russian

LAKE ONEGA

LAKE LADOGA

EUROPEAN RUSSIA

Moscow •

Tallinn
ESTONIA

Riga
LATVIA

LITHUANIA
Vilnius •

• Minsk

BELARUS

• Kiev

UKRAINE

SEA OF AZOV

Tblisi
GEORGIA

BLACK SEA

0 100 200 300 400 500 600 km
0 100 200 300 400 miles

INTRODUCTION

Europe is the birthplace of Western civilization. In the past, it dominated the world with science, industry and wealth. It is also a continent of constant change. During the twentieth century, two world wars and the collapse of communism changed Europe dramatically.

EARTHQUAKES AND VOLCANOES

Italy, Yugoslavia, Greece and Turkey lie on a fault line between two of the Earth's plates. Since the plates are constantly moving, these countries experience earthquakes and volcanoes.

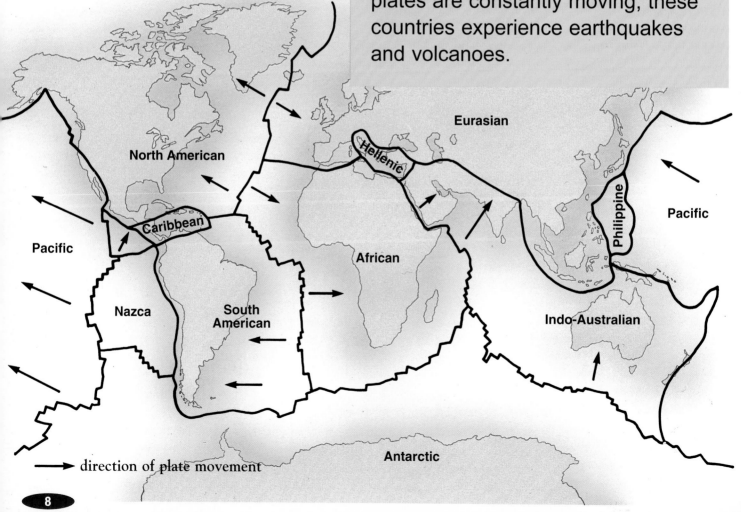

North American

Eurasian

Hellenic

Pacific

Philippine

Pacific

Caribbean

African

Nazca

South American

Indo-Australian

Antarctic

→ direction of plate movement

BIRTH OF A CONTINENT

Europe hasn't always been the shape it is now. Millions of years ago, the world looked very different. Europe was once joined to America.

About 150 million years ago, the continents gradually started to move apart. Where the Earth's plates crashed together, mountain ranges like the Grampians in Scotland and the Urals in Russia were formed.

Rivers have carved out valleys, wind and rain have eroded mountains, ice and frost have broken up rocks, and vast glaciers have gouged out landscapes.

Today, Europe's landscapes and the people who live on them are still changing.

150 MILLION

50 MILLION

◀ The globe 150 million years ago and 50 million years ago.

▼ The globe today.

LAND AND CLIMATE

Europe is smaller than every other continent except Australia. It covers an area of 10,531,623 km². Its population of almost 729 million people live in forty-seven countries, some of which have the highest population density in the world.

▲ Benidorm is a busy tourist resort in the Mediterranean.

SEAS

Europe's seas are sources of fish, gas and oil, and its coasts support an important tourist industry. The Mediterranean sea is the world's largest inland sea, reaching a depth of 5,000 metres. Its warm climate makes the Mediterranean region Europe's most popular tourist area.

The Black Sea is the size of Sweden. It reaches 2,210 metres deep and is useful to the countries that surround it.

The Baltic Sea is much shallower than the other seas, so it is easily polluted by industrial waste from eastern Europe.

POLLUTION AND WASTE

Carlo Ambretti runs a diving school in Sicily, on the Mediterranean coast. His business is in danger because underwater, everything is dying. Pollution from industry and new hotels are killing the coral and sponges that attract his customers. Divers used to see a colourful world on the seabed. Now everything is grey and lifeless.

▼ Yalta, a popular tourist resort on the Black Sea.

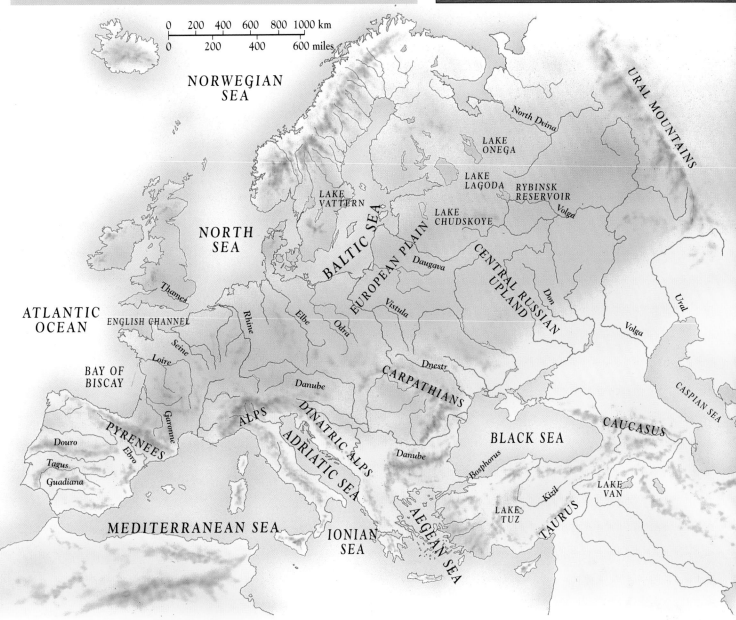

NORWEGIAN SEA

URAL MOUNTAINS

North Dvina

LAKE ONEGA

LAKE LAGODA

RYBINSK RESERVOIR

Volga

LAKE VATTERN

LAKE CHUDSKOYE

BALTIC SEA

EUROPEAN PLAIN

CENTRAL RUSSIAN UPLAND

NORTH SEA

Daugava

Don

Thames

Vistula

Volga

Urd

ATLANTIC OCEAN

ENGLISH CHANNEL

Rhine

Elbe

Odra

Seine

Dnestr

CASPIAN SEA

Loire

CARPATHIANS

BAY OF BISCAY

Danube

CAUCASUS

Garonne

ALPS

DINARIC ALPS

BLACK SEA

Douro

PYRENEES

Ebro

ADRIATIC SEA

Danube

Bosphorus

Tagus

Kizil

LAKE VAN

Guadiana

LAKE TUZ

TAURUS

MEDITERRANEAN SEA

IONIAN SEA

AEGEAN SEA

0   200   400   600   800 1000 km
0   200   400   600 miles

HIGHLANDS AND LOWLANDS

Mountains and valleys in north-west Europe give way to flat, rolling land in the east. Low mountains and high plateaus extend through the centre, and alpine mountain chains run across the south. The highest peak, Mount Elbrus, is 5,642 metres above sea-level in the Caucasus Mountains.

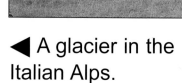

◀ A glacier in the Italian Alps.

▼ This diagram shows how a glacier gouges out valleys, while the melting ice forms rivers and lakes at the end.

Europe's great mountain chains were all formed by the Earth's crust moving together. The Scottish and Scandinvian highlands were formed first, over 200 million years ago. Later the Alps, Pyrenees, Carpathians and Sierra Nevada were formed.

Much of Europe is very low, too. Denmark's highest point is less than 17 metres above sea-level and 30 per cent of the Netherlands lies below sea-level.

▲ A storm surge barrier in the Netherlands, helping to protect flooding.

EARTHQUAKE IN TURKEY

On 21 August 1999, an earthquake measuring 7.4 on the Richter scale hit the town of Izmit in Turkey. The earthquake was the worst in Turkey in over 50 years and over 6,000 people died as hundreds of apartment blocks collapsed. The death toll was higher than it should have been because many of the apartment blocks were built recently using cheap, flimsy materials.

CLIMATE

Europe has many different climates. Countries close to the Atlantic have a moderate climate, with rain carried and dropped by winds from the ocean.

In eastern Europe, in the middle of the continent, temperatures can drop to $-12\,^{0}$C in the winter. The Mediterranean region is warmed by the sea, with hot summers and warm, wet winters.

AVERAGE TEMPERATURES

	Jan	July
Mediterranean	8 ^{0}C	22 ^{0}C
North-west Spain	12 ^{0}C	18 ^{0}C
Moscow	−12 ^{0}C	16 ^{0}C

▼ A deep fjord in Norway.

VEGETATION

Europe's vegetation is affected by climate and soil. In the far north, only moss, lichen and dwarf birch grow in the thin soil. In western and central Europe, trees and forests grow well in the warmer climate, although most has been cleared for timber and farming.

The Mediterranean has plants like olives, which do not need much water. But these plants decay slowly, so the soil is not very fertile.

Much of eastern Europe and Russia are covered in vast areas of prairie grass, or steppe. Further south, as it gets hotter, this can turn to scrubland or semi-desert.

▼ Types of vegetation in Europe.

Alpine and tundra
Mountain vegetation
Coniferous forest
Deciduous forest
Mixed forest
Grassland
Mediterranean
Scrub and semi-desert

EUROPE'S HISTORY

European history is a history of empire-building and power battles. But it is also a history of of political ideas, scientific discoveries, art, philosophy and religious beliefs, which have influenced the rest of the world.

▼ The exploration and trade routes of the fifteenth and sixteenth centuries.

The Greek and Roman Empires were the world's first great civilizations, between 500 BC until the late fourth century.

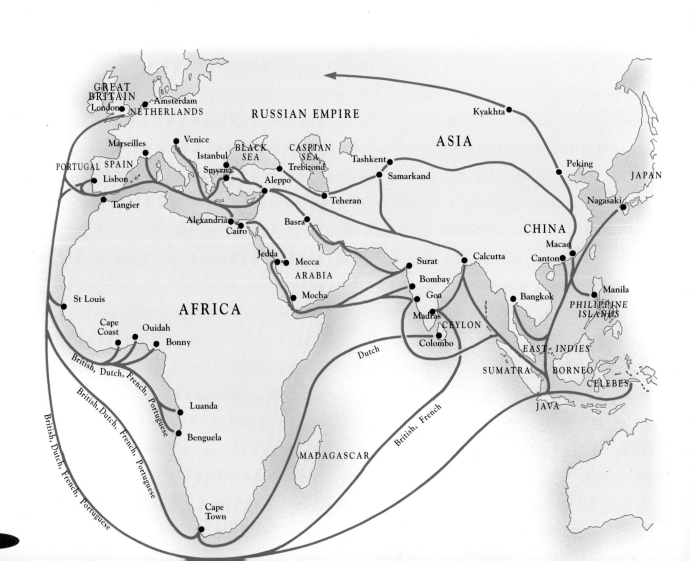

GREAT BRITAIN
London
Amsterdam
NETHERLANDS
RUSSIAN EMPIRE
Kyakhta
Marseilles
Venice
ASIA
BLACK SEA
CASPIAN SEA
Istanbul
Smyrna
Trebizond
Tashkent
Peking
PORTUGAL SPAIN
Lisbon
Aleppo
Samarkand
JAPAN
Tangier
Teheran
Nagasaki
Alexandria
Basra
CHINA
Cairo
Macao
Jedda
Surat
Calcutta
Canton
Mecca
Bombay
ARABIA
Goa
Manila
Mocha
Madras
Bangkok
PHILIPPINE ISLANDS
St Louis
CEYLON
AFRICA
Colombo
EAST INDIES
Cape Coast
Ouidah
Dutch
SUMATRA
BORNEO
Bonny
CELEBES
British, Dutch, French, Portuguese
JAVA
British, Dutch, French, Portuguese
Luanda
British, Dutch, French
Benguela
British, Dutch, French, Portuguese
MADAGASCAR
Cape Town

EMPIRE BUILDING

In the fifteenth and sixteenth centuries, Portuguese, Spanish and English sailors discovered sea routes to India, the West Indies and South America. They became valuable trade routes.

From the seventeenth to the nineteenth centuries, England, Spain, France and the Netherlands established colonies in Africa, India and East Asia. They grew sugar, cotton and tobacco using slaves from West Africa.

▲ The Cutty Sark is a sailing clipper which was used to carry goods such as tea.

▼ The European colonies at the end of the nineteenth century.

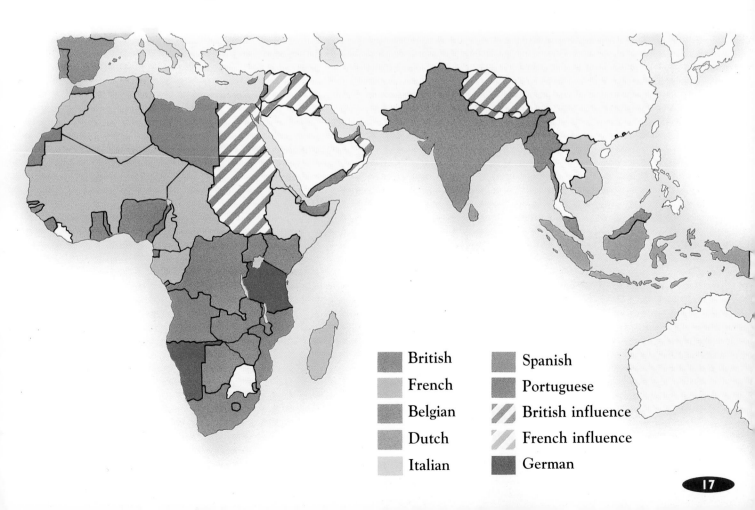

British

French

Belgian

Dutch

Italian

Spanish

Portuguese

British influence

French influence

German

WORLD WARS

From 1914–18, the First World War was fought between two powerful groups in Europe: Germany and Austria-Hungary on one side, and France, Russia and Britain on the other. In 1918, Germany and its allies surrendered, but the next twenty-one years saw Adolf Hitler's rise to power and Germany's preparation for war again.

In 1939, Germany invaded the former Czechoslovakia and Poland, and quickly conquered Norway, Denmark, Belgium, the Netherlands and Luxembourg. The Second World War began as Britain and its allies reacted.

▼ A picture taken on 2 November 1940 showing London buildings destroyed by German bombing air raids.

▲ Top: The Japanese bombing of the *USS Shaw*, in Pearl Harbour, 1941.

Below: US troops approaching the coast of France on D Day, 6 June 1944, when the allies re-invaded Europe.

JAPAN AND THE USA

In 1942, Japan entered the war in a pact with Germany. When Japan attacked a US fleet in Hawaii, the USA joined Britain and its allies. In 1945, Russian and allied troops approached Berlin from different sides and eventually Germany surrendered.

END OF COLONIALISM

Between 1947 and 1975, European colonies abroad gradually gained independence. But in many countries there was conflict and violence as new leaders took control.

THE IRON CURTAIN

Western bloc
Eastern bloc
Iron Curtain

▲ The Iron Curtain divided Eastern and Western Bloc countries.

▼ The Berlin Wall divided East and West Germany in Berlin.

EAST AND WEST

After the Second World War, Europe was split between communist countries in the East and non-communist countries in the West. The two sides were hostile towards each other over a period called the Cold War, although no actual fighting took place.

Eastern Europe, which consisted of the 'Eastern Bloc' countries and the Soviet Union, developed very differently from the West, with most decisions made by the government in Moscow.

In the 1980s, Mikhail Gorbachev, the leader of the Soviet Union, started allowing people greater choice and people across eastern Europe demanded free elections.

By 1991, democratic elections had been held in every eastern European country, including the Soviet Union. Non-communist parties in many countries had gained control of governments.

WESTERN PROBLEMS

The change from communism has been hard for many countries in eastern Europe. In some, such as the former Yugoslavia, the change has restarted old ethnic conflicts. Other countries, which have always been poorer, cannot compete with the West. They are starting to have problems of high crime rates and unemployment, which are typically 'Western' problems.

▼ Mikhail Gorbachev (left) was leader of the USSR from 1985-91 and leader of Russia until 2000.

PEOPLE

People in Europe have often been on the move, migrating from one region to another. Sadly, this has often been a result of religious or political persecution.

In the 1930s, Jews were persecuted by the Nazis in Germany. Millions of Jews died in concentration camps in Germany and Poland as the Nazi's tried to create a 'pure race'.

▲ A Jewish boy reads from the Torah.

▼ The main migrations of the twentieth century.

At the end of the First World War, new country boundaries were drawn up which ignored the ethnic groups within them. This meant different ethnic groups were scattered across eastern Europe. Some groups fled from new systems of government.

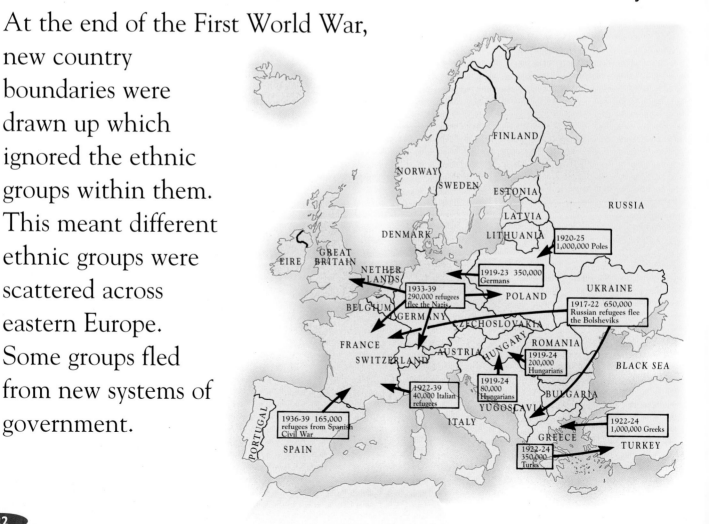

NORWAY
SWEDEN
FINLAND
ESTONIA
LATVIA
LITHUANIA
RUSSIA
DENMARK
EIRE
GREAT BRITAIN
NETHERLANDS
BELGIUM
GERMANY
POLAND
UKRAINE
CZECHOSLOVAKIA
FRANCE
SWITZERLAND
AUSTRIA
HUNGARY
ROMANIA
BLACK SEA
PORTUGAL
SPAIN
ITALY
YUGOSLAVIA
BULGARIA
GREECE
TURKEY

1920-25 1,000,000 Poles
1919-23 350,000 Germans
1933-39 290,000 refugees flee the Nazis
1917-22 650,000 Russian refugees flee the Bolsheviks
1919-24 200,000 Hungarians
1919-24 80,000 Hungarians
1922-39 40,000 Italian refugees
1936-39 165,000 refugees from Spanish Civil War
1922-24 1,000,000 Greeks
1922-24 350,000 Turks

BOSNIA AND KOSOVO

In 1991, the break-up of Yugoslavia resulted in bitter conflict between ethnic groups, first in Bosnia, in 1991, and later in Kosovo from 1998–99. Thousands of people were forced from their homes and killed, or driven out of the country as refugees.

▲ A Catholic pilgrims' mass in Spain.

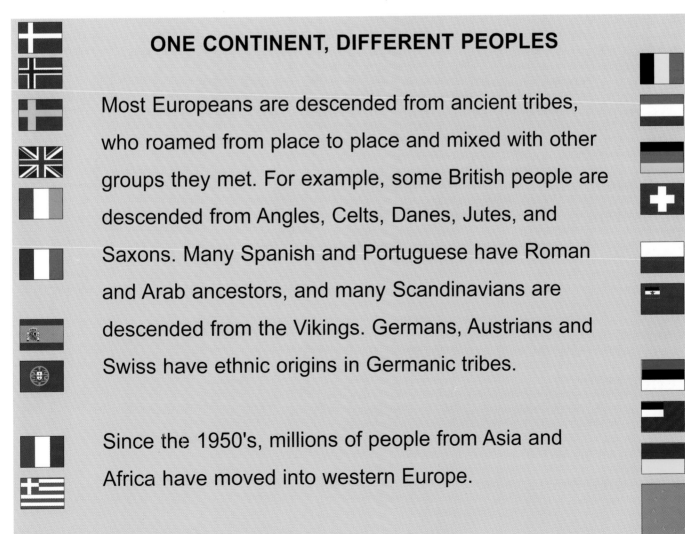

ONE CONTINENT, DIFFERENT PEOPLES

Most Europeans are descended from ancient tribes, who roamed from place to place and mixed with other groups they met. For example, some British people are descended from Angles, Celts, Danes, Jutes, and Saxons. Many Spanish and Portuguese have Roman and Arab ancestors, and many Scandinavians are descended from the Vikings. Germans, Austrians and Swiss have ethnic origins in Germanic tribes.

Since the 1950's, millions of people from Asia and Africa have moved into western Europe.

EUROPE TODAY

Europe is the most densely populated continent after Asia. Most people (over 73%) live in towns or cities, and have a high standard of living, with good health care, education and employment.

However, there are big differences between individual countries, and within the countries themselves.

▲ Europe's population densities.

Per mile²		Per km²
Over 500		Over 200
250-500		100-200
100-250		40-100
25-100		10-40
0-25		0-10

Northern European countries are generally richer than the south, because they are more industrialised. Rural areas are usually poorer than urban areas, but in the past twenty years, many city centres have grown poorer as people have moved out to the suburbs.

HEALTH CARE

Most Europeans have access to good health care. Death rates have fallen over the last twenty years as people have concentrated on living healthier lifestyles. But cancer, heart disease and road traffic accidents are still the major causes of death.

SLEEPING ROUGH

There are big differences between the rich and the poor in Europe. Homeless people sleep on the streets of some of Europe's wealthiest cities, including London, Paris and Rome.

Many used to have their own homes, but lost their jobs, often through no fault of their own. Now they cannot afford to pay rent and survive on handouts.

▼ A homeless man on the streets of Warsaw.

EDUCATION

Education levels are high in Europe. All children go to school, and 30 per cent of young people go to college or university.

In Italy and Portugal, children can leave school when they reach fourteen years. In Greece and Ireland, this rises to fifteen, and in Britain and Denmark it is sixteen. Over 97 per cent of adults can read and write.

▲ French engineering students.

▼ The *Tour de France* is a famous annual cycling race.

LEISURE-TIME

In most countries, spectator sports such as football are popular, and cable television now carries world matches into peoples' homes.

Other popular interests are food and drink, gardening, watching television and making home improvements.

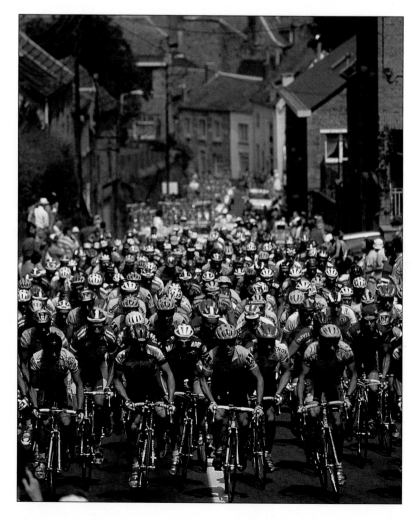

CULTURES

Every country is famous for a certain type of food or drink, art, music or fashion, which forms part of its national culture.

The French are well-known for their cafés, love of good food and fashion. In Greece and Italy, traditional society centred around the family is still important. Folk song, music, dance and bullfighting are part of Spain's national heritage.

Germany and Austria are famous for their beer, and Switzerland for its chocolate, cheeses and other dairy products.

In eastern Europe, Hungarian goulash, Polish sauerkraut and Czech beer are famous national symbols.

▲ A bullfight in southern Spain.

THE EUROPEAN UNION (EU)

The European Union (EU) is a partnership of European countries which co-operate on social, economic and political issues. It began in 1951 as a coal and steel partnership with just six countries, but now there are fifteen members, and others are waiting to join.

The EU works to increase its members' wealth by encouraging trade, and advises on ways to improve people's living and working conditions. It is also developing a foreign policy.

- ☐ 1957
- ☐ 1973
- ☐ 1981
- ☐ 1986
- ☐ 1995

▲ The fifteen members of the EU, with their date of joining.

MEMBERS OF THE EU

Date joined	Countries
1957	France, Italy, West Germany, Belgium, Luxembourg and the Netherlands.
1973	UK, Eire and Denmark
1981	Greece
1986	Portugal and Spain
1995	Austria, Sweden and Finland

WHO RUNS THE EUROPEAN UNION?

The EU is run by four major groups:

THE COUNCIL OF MINISTERS
All major decisions concerning the EU are made by the Council, which is made up of representatives of the governments of the member states. Twice a year, the heads of states themselves meet (eg. Britain's Prime Minister and France's President).

THE EUROPEAN COMMISSION
This group proposes legislation in areas such as agriculture, environment or transport.

THE EUROPEAN COURT OF JUSTICE
This is the supreme court of the EU. Its judgements must be obeyed by its members.

THE EUROPEAN PARLIAMENT
This group is made up of elected members (MEPs) from member states who meet for a week every month in Strasbourg. They cannot pass laws, but debate proposals.

▲ The building of the European Parliament, in Strasbourg.

SINGLE CURRENCY
On 1 January 1999, a single European currency, called the euro, became the official currency of eleven members of the EU, including France, Germany and Italy. The currency was created to help trade both within the EU and internationally.

RESOURCES

Europe is rich in natural resources such as coal, iron ore and gas. It is also a major manufacturing continent, turning raw materials into goods. Both raw materials and manufactured goods are exported abroad. EU countries are the highest exporters in the world, producing more than the USA. Eastern European industry, however, is far behind the West.

▼ An oil rig at Cromarty Firth in the North Sea, off the Scottish coast.

Europeans are big importers, as well as exporters, because they consume huge quantities of manufactured goods.

ENERGY AND POWER

Europe consumes vast amounts of energy, which cannot be replaced as quickly as it is consumed.

In the 1960s and 1970s, many countries developed nuclear power stations to try to produce more energy. But they were too expensive and dangerous to run, so most have been shut down.

The search is on to find alternative, renewable forms of energy, such as wind power or water power.

■ Tin
■ Iron ore
▲ Lead
▼ Bauxite
○ Copper
● Zinc
◉ Nickel
◇ Uranium
▽ Gold
△ Silver

▲ Europe's metal resources.

▼ A leukaemia ward in Kiev, close to the Chernobyl reactor.

CHERNOBYL

In 1986, a disastrous explosion and fire at the Chernobyl nuclear power plant in the Ukraine caused huge damage to the environment and to the local population. Radioactive pollution contaminated food and water supplies, and caused many health problems. Since 1986, many people in the area have developed cancer.

▼ Romanian farmers harvesting wheat with sickles. Some Eastern European countries are still not using farm machinery.

FOOD AND FARMING

Much of Europe is covered with rich soil, which helps produce vast quantities of crops. The continent exports millions of tonnes of food every year, especially cereal crops such as wheat, barley and oats.

In 1994, the EU was the fourth-largest producer of cereals in the world, after the USA, China and the former Soviet Union.

Other major crops include sugar beet, rye, potatoes and oilseed crops such as sunflowers, for products like margarine.

FOOD MOUNTAINS

Western Europe produces more food than it can sell at a good price, so the EU has set limits for farmers, called quotas, to keep food prices up. However, there are still surpluses of food and wine that are destroyed every year. Some people think this is wasteful.

Grazing animals are widespread in western Europe. Denmark and the Netherlands are specialist pig producers, Britain is a big sheep farmer and Mediterranean countries raise sheep and goats.

A WASTEFUL SYSTEM?

Jennifer Nicholson is a dairy farmer in southern England. Her cows often produce more milk than her EU quota allows, so she has to throw it away or allow her cows to 'go dry'. Jennifer says: "It seems a crazy system when you can't even give it away."

▼ In western Europe, machinery and the latest technology is used in farming.

CROP PRODUCTION IN EUROPE

TYPE OF CROP	PERCENTAGE OF COUNTRY'S TOTAL PRODUCTION			
	Europe	UK	Ireland	Italy
Cereals	10.9	16.2	5.3	8.1
Root crops	4.6	5.9	3.0	3.2
Industrial crops	3.6	2.8	0.2	3.9
Fruit & vegetables	14.2	10.8	3.0	7.5
Wine & olive oil	7.2	0.0	0.0	1.3
Flowers & plants	3.9	2.0	0.0	4.6
TOTAL	50	41	13.1	59.9

FORESTRY

Scandinavia and Russia both have major timber industries because they are covered with forest. In other countries such as Britain, forests are being made into places for recreation.

▲ Logs being moved in Sweden.

FISH

Fish off Europe's coasts provide work for both fishermen at sea and processing industries on land. There are often arguments between fishermen from different countries, who share the same seas and compete for the best catch.

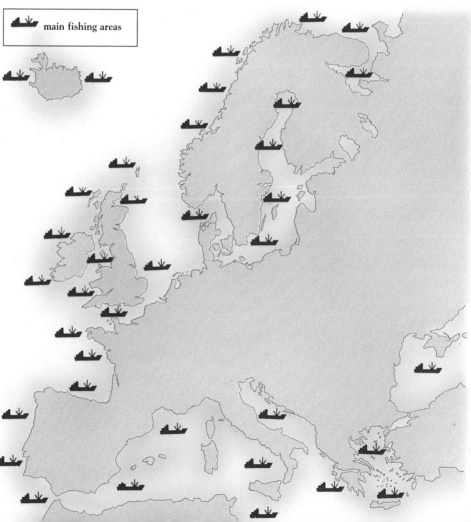

main fishing areas

▲ A fishing boat leaving a port in Norway, on its way out to sea.

OVER-FISHING

Fishing boats from EU countries can fish all around the continent, but modern fishing trawlers with enormous nets have over-fished the Atlantic and the North Sea.

There are now strict fish quotas limiting the amount of fish that can be taken from the seas, but some people are worried that the fish stocks will take years, if ever, to recover. One solution to over-fishing is fish farming – artificially rearing fish.

◄ A salmon fish farm in France. Norway produces over 115,000 tonnes of salmon a year.

A car factory in Germany. ▶
Car manufacturing is one of
Germany's major industries.

INDUSTRY

Manufacturing industries used to employ most Europeans until the 1980s. Since then, the fastest-growing industries in Europe have been service industries such as tourism, banking and insurance. In the 1990s, one of the fastest-growing service industries was the communications industry, including the internet.

MANUFACTURING INDUSTRIES IN EUROPE

- Food products 12.8%
- Electrical and electronic equipment 14.8%
- Cars, lorries, transport equipment 12.2%
- Chemicals 12%
- Machinery 10%
- Metal products 8.4%
- Textiles, clothing, leather and footwear 2.8%
- Paper, paper products, printing and publishing 7.6%
- Sand, gravel, precious stones, etc. 4.8%
- Rubber and processing of plastics 5.1%
- Metal-working industries 3.6%
- Timber and wooden furniture 3.2%
- Precision, optical and high technology instruments 1.5%
- Others 1.2%

COMMUTING

The increase in air traffic over the past thirty years has meant flying is getting cheaper and cheaper. Ulrich Christophersen often flies from his office in Norway to Germany for 2-hour meetings. "I can sort out problems on the spot, make decisions and plan ahead". By the afternoon he's back on a plane again.

LIFE IN A TRUCK

Helene Huber is a Dutch truck driver. She drives her own articulated lorry carrying 20-tonne containers all over Europe. Since some of her journeys take over a week, her lorry is equipped with sleeping accommodation. Border controls are so quick and easy within the European Union that Helene sometimes forgets which country she's travelling in.

Transport within Europe:
- By road 38%
- By sea 26.2%
- By inland waterways (canals and rivers) 18.4%
- By rail 6.8%
- By air 0.4%

TRANSPORT

The transport industry provides over 5% of Europe's employment. Most goods within Europe are carried by road, but air traffic has more than tripled over the past twenty-five years. The busiest airports in Europe are London, Paris and Frankfurt.

▼ TGV, the French high-speed train.

THE ENVIRONMENT

Industry, farming and Europe's population put great pressure on the natural environment. There is air and water pollution, and resources are used up quicker than they can be replaced.

◀ This lake in Scandinavia has been polluted by acid rain, which was carried by winds from western Europe.

WATER SUPPLIES

As towns and cities continue to grow in Europe, sewage and drainage systems exhaust the water supplies. In many regions, natural underground water is being used faster than it can be replaced, causing water shortages.

AIR POLLUTION

Harmful emissions from power stations and petrol vehicles are the main causes of pollution, especially in eastern Europe, where old technology is used in industry. Air pollution affects lakes, forests and damages the ozone layer in the Earth's atmosphere.

The EU is trying to cut air pollution by insisting that cars have catalytic converters, which lower harmful emissions.

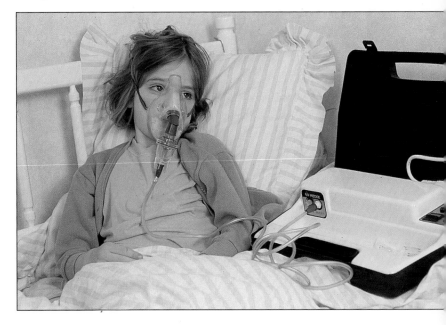

▲ There is a rising number of asthma sufferers in Europe as a result of the increase in air pollution.

◄ The harmful emissions from factories like this paper mill in Spain pollute the atmosphere.

WATER POLLUTION
Industry, farm pesticides, and sewage and rubbish from homes pollute the water, aswell as the air.

▲ A protected national park in Poland.

▼ Liquid waste is pumped on to Seaham Beach in England.

MAIN CAUSES OF PLANT EXTINCTION IN GERMANY

1. Changes in land use
2. Disappearance of rare sites
3. Landfill and urbanization
4. Disappearance of wetlands
5. Fertilizers
6. Mining and quarrying
7. Use of agricultural machinery
8. Maintenance and harnessing rivers
9. Air and soil pollution
10. Sewage and farm 'run off'

Many animals such as wolves, bears and wild boar used to live in Europe. They disappeared from the continent when their woodland habitat was destroyed.

Now, the EU is trying to protect certain species. For example, the Bird Directive requires member countries to try and protect over 175 species of birds and their habitats.

Air pollution ▶ has blackened this cathedral in France. The figure on the left has been cleaned.

HARMFUL TRADITIONS

Peter Micallef lives in a village in Malta. Every morning in April, he takes part in a traditional sport. He shoots songbirds as they migrate north. The Maltese government is trying to stop this tradition, because people in other parts of Europe think it is wrong. But old traditions can be very hard to change.

EUROPE IN THE WORLD

Today, Europe plays a smaller role in the world than it did in the past. But the continent is still a rich and powerful force.

The EU is the biggest exporter and importer of goods and services in the world, and as more countries join, it will grow even wealthier. Europe provides important aid to developing countries of the world, helping them improve people's standards of living. It is also a major contributor to relief agencies, helping victims of natural disasters or war.

▲ Clothes are handed out to refugees in Burundi.

▼ A UN team helps build a well in Liberia.

▲ This aircraft is a joint project between several European countries. The EU's defence policy will be an important issue over the next few years.

THE FUTURE

The future of Europe will be influenced by the development of the EU. In 1997, the Treaty of Amsterdam created new citizens' rights, which now apply to all its member states. Those laws, and the single currency, are intended to create a closer union among countries. Over the next ten years the Union could have an extra thirteen members from central and eastern Europe.

Some people are worried that they will lose their national identity by becoming too 'European'. They want to keep the differences between countries, not lose them. These are debates you can join, as new Europeans of the future.

TIMELINE

BC

6000 Farmers from Anatolia (now Turkey) reach Greece and Crete; farming spreads to northern and western Europe.

1900–1200 Mycenae Civilization established in Greece.

753 Founding of the Roman Empire.

500 Celts from central Europe reach Spain, Britain, Ireland and the Netherlands.

336–323 Alexander the Great conquers Persia (now Iran and Iraq) and establishes the Greek Empire as far as India, but it is broken up after his death.

AD

43–117 Romans conquer Britain; Roman Empire reaches its greatest extent.

449–457 Angles and Saxons from central Asia invade England.

700–960 Slavs (tribes of Indo-European origin) spread across eastern Europe, founding independent Slav states, including Poland, Russia, Croatia and Bulgaria.

793–800 Vikings from Scandinavia raid England; Charlemagne crowned Emperor of the Romans; his kingdom is later divided to form the basis of modern France and Germany.

871–899 Alfred the Great resists the advance of the Vikings and Danes in England; Norway established as independent country.

1337–1453 Hundred Years War between England and France, ending in English defeat. The Black Death (bubonic plague) kills a third of Europe (1347–1351).

1400–1500 The Renaissance, a period rich in literature and art, blooms in Europe.

1515–1534 Spanish conquistadors attack Mexico and Peru, destroying the Aztec and Inca civilizations

1517–1603 Reforms to the Roman Catholic Church, led by Martin Luther, lead to the Reformation and the creation of the Protestant Church in western Europe.

1618–1648 Thirty Years War involves most western European powers. Sweden, France and Brandenburg-Prussia (later Germany) emerge strengthened.

1650–1750 The Age of Reason or Enlightenment – a new respect for science and learning sweeps Europe.

1762–1796 Russia exerts increasing influence over eastern Europe. Advances in science and technology mark the beginning of the Industrial Revolution. The French Revolution (1789) begins; France becomes a republic and declares war on Austria and Prussia. Abolition of slavery. French troops, led by Napoleon Bonaparte, conquer much of Italy and Switzerland.

1813–1815 Napoleon defeated at the Battle of Waterloo by Britain and Prussia. Russia gains Finland from Sweden.

1850–1871 Prussia expands its territories to form a large united Germany under Kaiser Wilhelm I. Russia goes to war with Britain, France and Turkey over its claims over Turkey (Crimean War). Karl Marx publishes Das Kapital (1867) and establishes the ideas of communism.

1877–1914 Most of Africa colonized by European powers.

1908–1914 Unrest between Balkan countries and Austria-Hungary. Assassination of the Crown Prince of Austria by a Serbian triggers the First World War.

1917 Russian revolt against the ruling Tsar (Russian Revolution); Bolshevik party set up a communist regime.

1918 Germany surrenders to the allies; new nations become independent – the Baltic republics (Latvia, Estonia and Lithuania), Czechoslovakia and Yugoslavia.

1919 League of Nations set up to help preserve world peace.

1923–25 USSR formed. National Socialism (Fascism) emerges in Germany under Adolf Hitler and in Italy under Benito Mussolini.

1930–35 In Russia Stalin forces state ownership. Capitalist Europe enters the Great Depression. Fascist parties come to power in Italy, Germany and Spain. Germany begins the forced repatriation, and then murder of 'foreign nationals' and others, particularly communists and Jews.

1939–45 Hitler invades Czechoslovakia and Poland; Mussolini seizes Albania. Britain and France declare war on Germany and the Second World War begins. Germany finally defeated on 8 May 1945 and split into occupation zones.

1945–49 Europe divided into Eastern (Communist) and Western Blocs. Formation of NATO. European countries lose most of their overseas colonial powers

1951 European Coal and Steel Community formed between Belgium, France, Italy, Luxembourg, the Netherlands, and West Germany.

1955–56 Soviet Union signs the Warsaw Pact. Unrest in Hungary crushed by USSR.

1957–60 Treaty of Rome establishes the Common Market (EEC). Cyprus gains independence, but remains divided on Greek/Turkish lines.

1961 East Germany builds the Berlin Wall.

1968 Liberalization of Czechoslovakian communist party crushed by USSR. Revival of unrest in Northern Ireland between Protestants and Catholics.

1970 Unrest in Spain.

1980–85 Unrest in Poland led by Lech Walesa. Popular protests against nuclear weapons. USSR President Gorbachev introduces perestroyka (restructuring) and glasnost (openness).

1989–90 Poland and Hungary elect democratic governments. Popular uprisings in Czechoslovakia, East Germany and Bulgaria restore democracy, but in Romania there is a bloody revolt.

1990 Berlin Wall demolished and East and West Germany are reunited.

1991 Czechoslovakia divides into Slovakia and the Czech Republic.
Croatia, Slovenia, Macedonia and Bosnia-Herzegovina become independent from Yugoslavia. Civil war in Croatia and Bosnia. Soviet Union (USSR) dissolved.

1992 Maastricht Treaty signed by twelve European Community members and the European Union (EU) is formed.

1995 Sweden, Austria & Finland join the EU. War ends in Croatia. New Yugoslavia formed from Serbia and Montenegro.

1998 Conflict and violence in Kosovo.

1999 Launch of the euro (European single currency).

GLOSSARY

Allies Friends or partners. When used to describe the Second World War, allies refers to Britain, France and Russia.

Berlin Wall A wall that separated East and West Germany in Berlin. It was destroyed in 1989, when the countries were reunited.

Cold War A term describing the power struggle between the Communist world, led by the Soviet Union, and the non-Communist world, led by the USA, from the early 1950s to the 1970s.

Currency The money in use in a country or countries.

Democratic Chosen by the population of a country.

Ethnic conflicts Conflict over race.

Exported Sold abroad.

Foreign policy A plan of relationships with other countries.

Iron Curtain An imaginary line that divided Eastern and Western Bloc countries from the 1950s to the 1980s.

Imports Products bought from another country.

Independence When a colony becomes free from foreign rule.

Industrialised Countries which have developed manufacturing industries.

Migrating Moving to another place to live.

Moderate climate A climate that is neither very hot nor very cold.

Population density The amount of people living on a certain area of land, usually measured per square kilometre.

Raw materials Materials in their natural state, such as coal or iron ore.

Refugees People who have been forced out of their home country and are living abroad.

Resources Natural materials from a country, for example coal, iron ore, timber and fish.

TGV A French high-speed train which can travel up to 300 kph. The letters TGV stand for *trains a grande vitesse*.

FINDING OUT MORE

OTHER BOOKS TO READ

Ancient Greece and *Ancient Rome* (*History Beneath your Feet* series)(Hodder Wayland, 1999)

Atlas of Ancient Greece and Rome (Hodder Wayland, 1997)

Armistice, 1918 (*The World Wars* series) (Hodder Wayland, 2000)

The Berlin Wall (*New Perspectives* series)(Hodder Wayland, 1999)

Chernobyl and other Nuclear Accidents East Africa (*New Perspectives* series)(Hodder Wayland, 1999)

Eastern Europe (*World Fact Files* series)(Hodder Wayland, 1998)

France (*Country Fact Files* series)(Hodder Wayland, 1997)

Germany (*Country Fact Files* series)(Hodder Wayland, 1997)

Germany and Japan Attack (*The World Wars* series) (Hodder Wayland, 2000)

Great Battles of World War II (*The World Wars* series) (Hodder Wayland, 2000)

Leaders of World War II (*The World Wars* series) (Hodder Wayland, 2000)

My Childhood in Nazi Germany (Hodder Wayland, 1994)

The Rise of the Nazis (*New Perspectives* series)(Hodder Wayland, 1999)

Russia (*Country Fact Files* series)(Hodder Wayland, 1997)

Spain (*Country Fact Files* series)(Hodder Wayland, 1997)

Sweden (*Country Fact Files* series)(Hodder Wayland, 1997)

United Kingdom (*Country Fact Files* series)(Hodder Wayland, 1997)

The War in Former Yugoslavia (*New Perspectives* series)(Hodder Wayland, 1999)

The War in Kosovo (*New Perspectives* series)(Hodder Wayland, 1999)

The War in the Trenches (*The World Wars* series) (Hodder Wayland, 2000)

World War II: The Allied Victory (*The World Wars* series) (Hodder Wayland, 2000)

WEBSITES

The European Union: http://europa.eu.int

United Nations: http://www.undp.org

INDEX

Page numbers in **bold** show pictures as well as text.